Grace of God

A Journey of Faith, Hope, and Love

TABLE OF CONTENTS

Chapter 1:

A CHILLY SPRING NIGHT

March 2021:

The night was alive with the promise of change. A brisk breeze swept through the air, carrying the whispers of transformation on its wings. It was that magical time of year when winter reluctantly surrendered its icy grip, allowing spring to tiptoe in with tentative warmth. As I sat on the well-worn bleachers of the high school soccer field, I couldn't help but marvel at the palpable energy in the air.

My son was out there on the field, his passion for the game echoing in the cheers of the crowd. There was something enchanting about watching him play, about witnessing the fierce determination in his eyes as he weaved through the opposition, his footwork a dance of pure, unbridled dedication. The whole scene was alive with the rhythm of the game, the ball thudding against cleats, and shouts of encouragement echoing across the field.

But amid the joy of the game, a sudden pang of discomfort pulled me from my reverie. The chill in the air seemed to seep into my bones, a stark reminder that despite the promise of spring, winter's ghost still lingered. I wrapped my coat tighter around me, the fabric a feeble shield against the persistent cold.

As the match wore on, the air grew colder, and the stars began to peek out, casting their distant light upon the scene. The discomfort I felt, the persistent headache and a nagging cough, seemed insignificant compared to the camaraderie and unity that surrounded me. We were all here, a community bound by the shared passion of the game, united by the simple joy of witnessing our children chase their dreams across the field.

The chill that crept into my bones was not just a physical sensation; it was a foreshadowing of the challenges that lay ahead, challenges that would test not only my body but also the very core of my existence.

As the final whistle blew, marking the end of the game, a sense of pride swelled within me. My son's determination, his unwavering dedication, were a testament to the resilience that resided within him. With a mixture of exhaustion and exhilaration, we made our way home, the chill of the night still clinging to our skin.

That night, as I settled into bed, I hoped that the discomfort that had plagued me throughout the game would dissipate with rest. The warmth of the blankets covered me, a comforting contrast to the coldness that had surrounded us earlier.

Morning broke with a sliver of sunlight peeking through the curtains. But the promise of a new day was overshadowed by a heavy weight that seemed to settle upon my chest. Breathing, which had always been an involuntary and effortless act, now felt like a struggle. Each inhale was met with resistance, a reminder that something was amiss. Each cough felt worse.

With growing concern, I recognized that this was no ordinary discomfort. It was a signal, a clarion call from my body that something was wrong. Determined to seek answers, I made my way to an urgent care center, the air feeling heavy with each step.

The medical facility buzzed with activity, a microcosm of the world outside its walls. People shuffled in and out, their faces masked by a combination of hope and fear. The medical professionals moved with purpose; their dedication evident in every action. As I sat in the waiting room, the hum of conversations and the occasional burst of laughter served as a reminder that life, with all its uncertainties, continued to unfold.

The COVID-19 test was administered with a gentle efficiency, the nurse's gloved hands a testament to the caution that had become commonplace. And then, the waiting began – an agonizing hour that felt like an eternity. Time seemed to stretch, the seconds ticking away in slow motion as my mind raced through a series of possibilities.

Finally, the moment arrived, the nurse's expression a blend of empathy and gravity. Her words, delivered with a kindness that softened their impact, cut through the air. "I'm sorry to inform you, but your test results came back positive. You have contracted the virus."

The words hung in the air, a weighty declaration that reverberated within me. The virus that had brought the world to its knees, the invisible adversary that had dominated headlines and conversations, had found its way to me. In that moment, the ordinary became extraordinary. The discomfort that had been a footnote to the soccer game now took on a new meaning – it was a symptom, a signal of the battle that would unfold within my body.

As I left the urgent care center, the weight of the diagnosis settled upon my shoulders. The chill of the spring night seemed to have seeped into my bones, a metaphor for the uncertainty that now marked my journey. Little did I know that this was just the beginning, that the journey ahead would test my resilience, challenge my beliefs, and reshape my understanding of the world around me.

Chapter 2:

BATTLING THE INVISIBLE ENEMY

In the midst of uncertainty, my wife emerged as a beacon of strength. With unwavering determination, she embarked on a mission to safeguard our home, to fortify the very walls that had witnessed our joys and sorrows. Armed with disinfectants and a heart full of love, she meticulously sanitized every surface, every nook and cranny, waging a war against an invisible adversary. Her efforts were not just an act of protection; they were a testament to the power of love, a love that was unyielding in the face of adversity.

As the echoes of her disinfecting fervor reverberated through the air, I found myself confined to the confines of our basement. The isolation was a stark reminder of the reality that had taken hold of my life. Days stretched into each other, merging into a blur of discomfort and solitude. I was engaged in a battle against an enemy I couldn't see, an enemy that had infiltrated not just my body but also my sense of security.

The symptoms were relentless, a constant reminder that I was engaged in a fight for my well-being. The fever burned within me, a fire that consumed my strength and resolve. The simple act of breathing, once taken for granted, had transformed into a laborious effort. Each inhale was a battle, an internal struggle against an invisible force that sought to deprive me of the very life force that sustained me.

In those moments of weakness, my wife's care was a lifeline. She appeared like an angel of nourishment, carrying bowls of soups that offered comfort and sustenance. The aroma of the broth, the warmth that seeped into my bones, became a balm for both body and soul. The nourishment she provided was not just physical; it was a manifestation of her unwavering support, a testament to her determination to stand by my side in the face of adversity.

Water, too, became a source of solace. Each sip was a reminder that life persisted, that even during a battle against an invisible enemy, the basic rhythms of existence continued. And in the quiet moments, when pain and discomfort took a temporary respite, I found solace in the pages of books that transported me to different worlds. They offered an escape, a respite from the relentless battle that waged within me.

Hours turned into days, and the calendar became a mute witness to the relentless passage of time. The support of loved ones, my parents, my sister, though physically distant, served as a lifeline that connected me to a world beyond the confines of my basement sanctuary. Phone calls, texts, and video chats with my doctor were threads that tied me to the tapestry of life, reminding me that I was not alone in this battle.

Yet, despite the care and the remote support, the virus refused to release its grip. My oxygen levels, once stable, became a source of growing concern. The numbers on the monitor, once insignificant, now held the power to stir anxiety within me. 94, 91, 88 – each drop in oxygen levels felt like a step closer to the precipice. Fear, like an uninvited guest, settled in the corners of my mind, a constant companion that whispered doubts and uncertainties.

The future, once a canvas of possibilities, now seemed shrouded in a haze of ambiguity. Would I emerge from this trial with my strength intact? Would my body find the resilience to fight back against the invisible foe that had laid claim to it? The questions swirled within me, each one carrying the weight of a world that had been upended.

But amid the darkness, a glimmer of hope emerged – the unwavering determination to overcome. As I lay in the quiet of my isolation, I drew strength from the love that surrounded me. The love of my wife, who stood as a pillar of support, and my children who were checking in on me via text. The love of my family, who cheered me on from afar. The love that resided within me, a reservoir of resilience that had been ignited by the challenge I faced.

And so, with each labored breath, with each moment of discomfort, I summoned the spirit of a warrior. The battle against the invisible enemy raged on, but within me burned a fire that refused to be extinguished. The days might have been challenging, the future might have been uncertain, but the spirit of perseverance held firm. I was engaged in a battle, a battle not just for my physical well-being, but for the very essence of who I was.

Chapter 3:

DESPERATION AND UNCERTAINTY

As my oxygen levels continued their downward spiral, fevers were getting higher, a sense of desperation took hold, gripping my consciousness like a vise. It became evident that seeking immediate medical attention was my only hope. I texted my wife, who was upstairs cooking dinner, that I felt worse and I'm going to the hospital. She said "OK, do you need me to take you? I said "No, I'll drive myself". I got dressed and mustered every ounce of strength to make my way to the hospital, driven by the primal instinct to survive. The world outside seemed to blur as I stumbled towards my car, my steps faltering, yet resolute.

When I arrived at the hospital, I was met by a scene of overwhelming chaos. The hospital's fluorescent lights flickered overhead, casting an eerie glow that seemed to mirror the uncertainty that gripped my heart. Each step I took down the sterile corridors was a testament to my sheer willpower, a determination to seek the help that had become my lifeline. The rhythmic beeping of monitors and the hushed voices of medical staff provided a dissonant soundtrack to my internal turmoil.

Entering the reception area felt like crossing a threshold into a different realm, a world where time seemed to stretch and warp. The receptionist, a distant figure shrouded in her own concerns, barely looked up as I approached. It was as if my presence was just another detail in a script that had been written long before this moment. I cleared my throat, my voice betraying the desperation that churned within me.

"I have covid and I need help," I managed to say, my words a plea that hung heavily in the air. The receptionist's gaze finally lifted from the computer screen, her eyes meeting mine with a mixture of confusion and curiosity. She hesitated for a moment, the weight of my situation apparent in the furrow of her brow.

"COVID-19 positive, and I don't know why he's here," she mumbled more to herself than to me, her fingers dancing across the keyboard as she verified my status. The seconds that ticked by were excruciating, each one carrying with it the weight of my deteriorating condition. Finally, she looked up, her expression shifting from detachment to a hint of concern. "Sir, please take a seat. We'll get to you as soon as we can."

The chairs in the waiting area were an uncomfortable reminder of the situation at hand. As I settled into one, the sterile plastic cool against my skin, a swirl of thoughts engulfed me. The minutes stretched into an eternity, and every tick of the clock on the wall seemed to echo the thud of my racing heart. My mind was a whirlwind of fears and scenarios – the possibility of waiting hours, of my condition worsening while I sat here, of not receiving the care I so desperately needed.

Hours dragged on, each minute feeling like an eternity as I remained seated, my strength waning, frustration and anxiety bubbling to the surface. I prayed fervently for a glimmer of hope, a sign that relief was imminent. Yet, my oxygen levels remained perilously low, and the fear of further deterioration weighed heavily on my mind. With every passing second, the flicker of hope dimmed, and I began to wonder if my plea for help would go unanswered.

In a moment of both desperation and courage, I made the difficult decision to leave the hospital and return home. The risk of the hospital's uncertain timeline loomed large, and the perilously low levels of oxygen in my body meant that waiting was no longer an option. If I was going to pass, I didn't want it to be in a hospital; I'd rather it be at home close to my family. As I descended back into the isolation of our basement, a heavy cloak of uncertainty settled over me. I texted my family members that I loved them.

Chapter 4

THE DARKNESS BEFORE DAWN

Time marched forward, days blending into weeks as I continued to grapple with the relentless grip of COVID-19. The battle showed no signs of abating, and I confronted fevers that felt like wildfires scorching my body, weakness that rendered even the simplest tasks herculean, and a constant reminder of my compromised oxygen levels that left me gasping for breath. I prayed to God several times, begging for the strength to endure.

The passage of time felt interminable, each tick of the clock a reminder of the arduous journey I was traversing. Yet, even in the midst of this seemingly unending ordeal, there were moments that pierced through the darkness like stars in a night sky. One morning, I awoke without a fever, and a surge of excitement coursed through me like a burst of energy. With haste, I fumbled for my phone and texted my wife the news – a promising sign that perhaps the tide was beginning to turn. Her response, a cascade of joyful emojis and words of encouragement, echoed the hope that was slowly taking root within me.

With each passing day, my body responded more positively to the battle I waged against the invisible adversary. My oxygen levels, which had plummeted to worrisome lows that left me feeling like I was drowning on land, gradually began their ascent, like a phoenix rising from the ashes. Though physically weakened, a renewed sense of determination pulsed through my veins, as if my body and mind were aligning in a harmonious symphony of resilience.

The mental fog that had enveloped me, a dense shroud that dulled my thoughts and clouded my perceptions, began to lift. Like the gradual clearing of mist after a long night, my mind became sharper, more focused, and I caught a glimpse of a flickering light at the end of the seemingly endless tunnel I had been navigating. It was as if I had been submerged in a sea of uncertainty, and now, finally, my head had breached the surface, allowing me to breathe in the promise of better days.

During those days of recovery, as I stepped outside and felt the warmth of the sun on my skin, I reflected on the journey that had brought me to this point. It was a journey marked by fear, desperation, and uncertainty, but also one illuminated by the strength of the human spirit and the unwavering support of loved ones. The lessons I had learned were etched into my being – the fragility of life, the power of hope, and the resilience that can be found even in the darkest of times.

One particularly poignant connection was through my son's high school soccer games while I was in the basement. Although I couldn't physically be present at the field, I watched his games through my phone, my cheers joining the virtual chorus of support from afar. Each kick of the ball, each goal scored, was a reminder that life was still moving forward, that the spirit of determination and passion persisted even in the face of adversity. The games provided a sense of continuity, a link to normalcy in a time that had been defined by upheaval.

The world outside continued to evolve, the pandemic's grip slowly loosening as vaccines and medical advancements offered a glimmer of relief. But within the walls of my home, I was engaged in a battle that was uniquely my own, a battle that transcended statistics and headlines. It was a battle not just against a virus, but against the depths of my own fears and limitations. Each step forward, each labored breath turned triumphant, was a victory that reinforced my determination to overcome. The dawn, though distant, was no longer a mere glimmer but a tangible beacon of hope.

Chapter 5:

A GLIMPSE OF VICTORY

April 2021:

As my journey of recovery continued, I found myself navigating a new rhythm of life – one that was marked by both the challenges of healing and the gifts of introspection. The isolation that had once felt stifling began to transform into a cocoon of self-discovery, a space where I could reflect on the fragility of life and the depth of my own resilience.

The days no longer stretched on endlessly; instead, they took on a cadence that was measured by progress. With each step I took, each improvement in my health, I found myself inching closer to a sense of normalcy. The simple acts that had once been taken for granted – taking a deep breath, walking up the stairs without feeling winded, savoring a meal without the weight of illness – became moments of triumph that filled me with gratitude.

Walking our dog, an activity that had once been a part of my pre-COVID daily routine, took on a new significance. Each step I took with my faithful companion was a testament to the progress I was making, a physical manifestation of my journey from weakness to strength. The rustling of leaves beneath my feet, the fresh air that filled my lungs, and the wagging tail beside me were all reminders that life's simplest pleasures held a profound beauty.

As I looked back on the arduous journey I had undertaken, a profound sense of gratitude washed over me like a soothing balm. I had confronted one of the greatest challenges of my life and emerged victorious on the other side. Though exhausted and weathered by the unrelenting storm of uncertainty, I returned to the rhythm of my normal life, having depleted all the accrued time off from work due to the relentless virus. The road to recovery had been long, fraught with seemingly insurmountable obstacles, but the experience had transformed me in ways I could never have imagined, etching its indelible mark upon the fabric of my being.

Once I was able to taste again, a morning cup of coffee had never been so gratifying as it was during those days when every sip felt like a celebration of life itself. Each step I took was a testament to the resilience of the human body and spirit, a reminder that even when faced with seemingly insurmountable odds, we have the capacity to heal, to overcome, and to emerge stronger than before. The mundane aspects of life that I had once taken for granted now carried a weight of profound significance – a warm embrace, the laughter of my children and grandchildren, the simple pleasure of feeling the sun's gentle caress on my skin.

In returning to work, I found myself greeted by both admiration and empathy from colleagues who had followed my journey from a distance. Their encouraging words and warm embraces were a reminder that the bonds that connect us as humans can become even stronger in the face of adversity. And as I settled back into my routine, I carried with me not only the scars of battle but also a newfound reservoir of inner strength.

The road to recovery had been long and fraught with obstacles, but the experience had transformed me in ways I could never have imagined, forging in the crucible of adversity a spirit unbreakable and a gratitude for life's simplest joys unparalleled. This was a chapter in my life that would forever resonate as a testament to the resilience of the human spirit.

Chapter 6:

NEW DAYS

The sun's gentle rays streamed through the window on that beautiful spring morning, casting a warm and inviting glow across the room. The aroma of freshly brewed coffee wafted through the air, intertwining with the soft chirping of birds outside. As I sat at the kitchen table, cradling my mug in my hands, I couldn't help but marvel at the simple pleasures that life had to offer – the quiet stillness of the morning, the promise of a new day, and the comfort of routine. Little did I know that this seemingly ordinary day held within its grasp an extraordinary surprise that would forever alter the course of our lives.

At the age of 44, I found myself in a phase of life where my roles had expanded to encompass not only that of a father to three grown children but also that of a proud grandfather to my grandchildren. The walls of our home echoed with the laughter and joy that our family gatherings brought, each moment etching itself into the tapestry of our shared memories. Our lives were woven together by threads of love, and the bonds between us grew stronger with each passing day. Our home was a sanctuary of togetherness, a haven where generations mingled, and stories were passed down like cherished heirlooms.

Yet, as the saying goes, fate has a way of interjecting its presence when least expected. It was on this ordinary morning, with my coffee mug warm in my hands, that destiny was poised to unfold yet another chapter of our family's journey. The events that were about to transpire would test our collective strength, redefine the contours of our love, and inspire us to face the unknown with unwavering resolve.

As the morning light painted intricate patterns on the floor, I contemplated the significance of family. Our shared experiences, our dreams, and the unconditional love that bound us together were the foundations upon which we built our lives. We reveled in the present, celebrating milestones and achievements, while also looking toward the future with hope and anticipation. Our family unit was a fortress, a place of refuge from life's storms, and I took solace in the fact that we were a beacon of support for one another.

But, as if guided by an invisible hand, fate had woven another thread into the tapestry of our lives. A thread that would test the very fibers of our strength and resilience and challenge us to embrace the unexpected with open hearts. The spring breeze that rustled the curtains carried with it a whisper of change, a harbinger of the twists and turns that awaited us on the horizon.

The tranquility of that morning was about to give way to a storm, the likes of which our family had never before encountered. Yet, amid the turbulence, we would discover depths of courage and unity we never knew we possessed. This was the dawning of a new chapter, one that would test our bonds and illuminate the resilience of the human spirit.

Chapter 7:

THE UNEXPECTED NEWS

May 2021:

The days flowed in their usual rhythm, with life's demands and routines occupying our time. It was during one of these seemingly ordinary days that my phone rang, the familiar tune of my wife's call breaking the silence. I answered, my voice infused with curiosity, "Hey, what's up?" Her reply, however, was anything but ordinary. "Guess what?" she asked, her tone a mixture of excitement and something else – something I couldn't quite decipher. A playful response slipped from my lips, "Did you get a raise at work?" A brief pause followed, "No," she said, her voice tinged with a touch of disbelief, "our daughter is pregnant. We will be welcoming our third grandchild 6 months from now." The enormity of what she had just said took a moment to sink in. This was not a dream; it was not a playful jest. Our daughter was pregnant, and we were about to embark on a new chapter of our family's story.

As the realization settled over me, a mixture of emotions surged within. Joy, surprise, and a touch of apprehension danced in a delicate balance. We were about to enjoy the company of another rascal running around the house. The news was both unexpected and exciting, and it cast a new light on our family's dynamics.

Just a week later, another unexpected twist rewrote the narrative of our lives once again. My wife sat me down, her eyes dancing with a mix of emotions that I'd come to recognize. She took a deep breath and said, "I'm pregnant." The words hung in the air, a revelation that seemed almost surreal in its timing. Our family was expanding not just in one direction, but in multiple dimensions, weaving a tapestry of interconnected stories that were uniquely ours. The joy and complexity of these new realities cascaded over us, mingling with the uncertainties that had already taken root. We were navigating uncharted territory – supporting our daughter through her pregnancy while simultaneously preparing to welcome a new addition to our family. The emotions were a whirlwind, a blend of excitement, apprehension, and an overwhelming sense of responsibility.

In the span of mere weeks, our lives had been reshaped by these extraordinary developments. Amid the fear and challenges, a profound sense of love and purpose emerged, strengthening our resolve to face whatever lay ahead. As we embraced these unexpected chapters, we knew that our story was still being written. The pages were filled with emotions, challenges, and moments of connection that would shape our lives in ways we couldn't yet imagine. Our family was expanding, not just in numbers, but in depth and meaning, and we were ready to face this new chapter with open hearts and a steadfast determination to cherish every moment along the way. We were seasoned parents, familiar with the challenges and joys of raising children, yet the idea of adding another member to our family stirred a mixture of excitement and uncertainty. But little did we know that a different kind of plot twist was waiting just around the corner.

Chapter 8

THE CALL

A call from the doctor's office, like a bolt from the blue, altered the trajectory of our journey. The urgency in the doctor's voice was palpable, and they requested an immediate Zoom call. Anxiety churned within us as we hurriedly set up the virtual meeting. As the call commenced, the doctor's face appeared on the screen, their expression a blend of professionalism and empathy. They began to speak, their words measured and careful, conveying mostly concerns. The doctor's words hung heavy in the air as they delicately broached the topic of disabilities, including trisomy 21 and others, that our unborn child would most likely face.

The gravity of their words sank deep into our souls, leaving us with a flood of emotions. As tears streamed down our faces, the doctor compassionately asked us a question that would shape the path ahead: "How would you like to proceed, considering it is still early in the pregnancy?" The weight of this decision, coupled with the revelation that we were expecting a girl, intensified the waves of emotions crashing over us. Fear, sadness, and an overwhelming sense of helplessness washed over our hearts, as we struggled to envision a future that seemed clouded by adversity. The once clear horizon of our dreams now seemed obscured, as we faced the uncertainty that laid ahead.

In that defining moment, though our hearts ached, and uncertainty loomed, we knew deep within our souls that terminating the pregnancy was not an option, no matter how overwhelming the odds seemed. Guided by an unwavering faith and an unyielding belief in the extraordinary power of love, my wife and I made a unanimous decision—to proceed with the pregnancy, no matter what happens. We chose to stand by our little girl, embracing her regardless of the challenges she might face.

With tear-stained faces, we concluded the Zoom call that had ushered in a new era of uncertainty. The doctor's words hung in the air, heavy and poignant, a stark reminder of the challenges ahead. Yet, as we looked into each other's eyes, the bond that had carried us through life's trials shone brightly. Love, that unwavering anchor, held us steady amid the storm.

In the wake of that emotional call, I retreated to the kitchen, my footsteps a quiet cadence against the floor. I opened a drawer, retrieved a plain piece of paper, and grasped a marker. With resolute strokes, I wrote "Grace of God" on the paper and showed it to my wife. It was a simple phrase, but its significance resonated deep within us. It became more than just words on paper; it became a beacon of light, a talisman of hope that we could hold onto as we navigated the unpredictable path before us.

As the days unfolded, our lives transformed into a whirlwind of hospital visits and medical consultations. Time seemed to blur as we moved from one appointment to the next, each one bringing with it a fresh set of tests and procedures. The hospital, once a distant place, became a realm we became intimately acquainted with. Our hour-long car journeys to the hospital were marked by a mix of anticipation and trepidation, our hands intertwined as we faced the unknown together.

During one of these visits, I found myself seated in the ultrasound room, the monitors before me displaying a dance of lines and shapes. The room was hushed, the air charged with a sense of reverence. My wife laying on the examination bed, her expression a blend of hope and uncertainty. The technician's hands moved deftly, the ultrasound wand gliding over her abdomen.

And then, as if a symphony of life itself, a sound emerged from the speakers – the delicate, rhythmic cadence of a heartbeat. It was the heartbeat of our unborn daughter, a sound that reverberated through the room and seemed to echo within the very chambers of my heart. In that moment, time seemed to pause. The worries, the fears, the weight of uncertainty – all faded into the background, overshadowed by the sheer miracle unfolding before us.

Tears pricked at the corners of my eyes as I listened to that steady rhythm. It was a song of life, a testament to resilience, and a reminder that even in the face of adversity, beauty and hope persisted. The heartbeat was a tangible connection, a lifeline that stretched between our daughter and us, reminding us of the precious life that was taking shape within my wife's womb.

In the midst of medical jargon, tests, and procedures, that heartbeat became our compass. It guided us through the maze of uncertainty, providing us with a sense of direction and purpose. Each week brought new challenges, new information, and new decisions to be made. Yet, as we navigated this labyrinth, the "Grace of God" card remained a constant presence – a symbol of the strength that love, hope, and faith can bestow upon a family in their darkest hours.

Chapter 9:

THE HEART'S SYMPHONY

As the days melted into weeks, the rhythm of time accompanied us on our remarkable journey, each tick of the clock a poignant reminder of the impending moment when our lives would change forever. During uncertainty, our embraces became silent prayers, every ultrasound, and each heartbeat serving as a glimpse into the resilient life taking shape within my wife's womb. During one particular ultrasound, the specialist's words held a touch of surprise and wonder as she remarked, "Wow, she has a lot of hair." It was a moment that sparked smiles and warm embraces, a reminder that even during challenges, there were joyful surprises to be found.

In that moment, our world was contained within the small examination room, our hearts echoing with the reassurance that we were not alone on this journey. Our faith had been our constant companion, our guide through the uncharted waters that lay ahead. With every ultrasound image, we felt a connection, an unbreakable thread weaving between us and our daughter. She was our beacon of hope, a testament to the strength of the human spirit and the power of love.

However, as we were about to learn, our journey was far from over. More challenges awaited us, each one a test of our resolve and a chance to reaffirm our faith. But in those fleeting moments of joy and anticipation, we held onto the belief that no matter what hardships came our way, the grace of God would always be there to light our path.

A turning point arrived when my wife received a call for a meeting with the doctor. My mother-in-law accompanied her to the hospital, a pillar of support in these critical moments. The doctor, his demeanor calm and reassuring, explained his recommendation – an amniocentesis test. This procedure, while potentially risky, held the promise of delivering crucial information about our baby's well-being.

As they sat in the consultation room, a mix of hope and apprehension swirled in the air. The doctor's words were measured, his explanations clear as he detailed the procedure and its purpose. Amniotic fluid would be delicately extracted from the womb, a procedure that could provide valuable insights into any genetic abnormalities or potential birth defects. While the doctor's words were factual, my wife's emotions soared and dipped like waves on a stormy sea.

Tears flowed freely down her cheeks as she confronted the weight of what this procedure could reveal. The doctor's reassuring words did little to silence the thunder of her fears – the potential risks, the uncertainties of the results, and the emotional whirlwind that could follow. Beside her, my mother-in-law offered a steady presence, her unwavering support a lifeline in the storm. The doctor's reassurances and explanations, while vital, couldn't dispel the raw vulnerability my wife felt. The decision ahead was profound, and the emotions stirred by it were complex and intense. Facing the unknown, the future of our unborn child seemed suspended in a moment of anticipation.

Regardless of the results obtained from the amniocentesis, it is essential to acknowledge the emotional journey that my wife underwent during this process. Providing her with unwavering support, empathy, and understanding is crucial, as that played a significant role in helping her process and cope with the emotions that emerged. Together, we can navigate through the uncertainties, bask in the joy, and hope that comes with this precious phase of our lives.

Chapter 10:

HEARTBEAT

As we reached a little past the midpoint of my wife's pregnancy, a time that should have been brimming with anticipation and joy, fate had other plans for us. Our journey, already marked by challenges, took an unexpected turn. It was during a routine visit to the hospital for our weekly check-in that the veil of uncertainty descended upon us once again. The doctor's words hung in the air like a heavy cloud as they delivered the crushing news of a ventricular septal defect (VSD) in our unborn daughter's heart. The weight of that diagnosis settled like a boulder in our chests, leaving us breathless and bewildered. In a world that had already tested our strength and resilience, this news was a seismic jolt that rocked the foundation of our hopes and dreams. Our journey to parenthood, which had been a tapestry of hope and determination, was now interwoven with threads of fear and uncertainty.

Amid this storm, our focus shifted entirely. Joyful thoughts of nursery decorations and baby showers gave way to a laser-like attention on our baby girl's heart defect, the intricate organ that held the key to her well-being. The shadow of potential surgery loomed over us, a specter that had previously seemed confined to medical dramas on television. Now, it was a real and daunting prospect, one that we had never imagined we would have to grapple with.

Days turned into weeks, and each day brought a new mix of emotions. Hope and fear danced an intricate ballet within our hearts as we awaited updates on the condition of the hole in our daughter's heart. The possibility of it growing larger became a haunting presence, a constant reminder of the fragility of life. We immersed ourselves in learning about ventricular septal defects, the medical procedures, and the possibilities that lay ahead.

But even in the darkest of times, there was a flicker of light. Our faith, unwavering and resolute, became our guiding star. It was in the quiet moments of prayer and reflection that we found solace, a way to anchor ourselves amidst the storm. We clung to the belief that our daughter was a precious gift, a testament to the strength of love and the resilience of the human spirit. As we ventured into the unknown territory of VSD, we quickly realized that we were not alone on this journey. Our family, friends, and faith community enveloped us in a cocoon of support and love. Each message of encouragement, every shared prayer, was a reminder that even in the face of adversity, we were part of a larger tapestry of humanity, bound together by our capacity to care.

During uncertainty, we found strength. Amid fear, we found hope. And as we held onto each other, we also held onto the belief that our daughter's heart, fragile as it may be, was a symbol of resilience and a testament to the power of love. As we continued to navigate the uncharted waters of VSD, we were reminded that every heartbeat was a precious symphony, a melody of life that resonated with courage, determination, and an unbreakable bond. In the heart's symphony, we found the strength to face the challenges that lay ahead, knowing that love would guide us through.

Chapter 11:

HOLDING ON TO HOPE

The days unfurled like an unending tapestry; each one marked by a blend of emotions that swirled through the corridors of our hearts. Time became a river, carrying with it the ebb and flow of hope and trepidation. Every heartbeat, every ultrasound, and every medical update transformed into a symphony of anticipation and anxiety. The waiting room of the hospital became a realm of shared humanity, a place where stories of courage and resilience intersected with the fabric of our own.

In those hushed moments of waiting, I found myself drawn into a sea of contemplation. The journey that had led us to this point felt like a novel itself—a narrative of strength, hope, and love. What had started as a battle against an invisible enemy had now transformed into a fight for our daughter's future. The hurdles we had overcome hadn't just tested our mettle; they had forged an unbreakable bond and fortified our belief in the boundless power of love.

With the due date looming on the horizon, a crescendo of emotions surged within us. Excitement intermingled with anxiety, creating a kaleidoscope of feelings that painted our days. We knew that the path ahead was paved with uncertainties, but within the chambers of our hearts, we held steadfast to the unwavering truth that our daughter was a precious gift, a jewel to be cherished regardless of the challenges that awaited her. Each night, as I rested in the stillness, I sent whispers of hope into the universe, a silent plea for her well-being that transcended words.

And then, like a sudden thunderclap, the call shattered the fragile tranquility that had settled around us. The news arrived, unexpected and urgent—a stark revelation that my wife's placenta was faltering, demanding an emergency C-section two weeks ahead of schedule. In that moment, fear surged through me, a torrent that threatened to engulf reason. The unknown stretched before us like an uncharted abyss, and my thoughts spun with a vortex of worst-case scenarios. Amid the tumult, we rallied our closest friends and family, delivering the news that our journey had taken an unforeseen turn and that we were bound for the hospital.

The drive to the hospital was a blur of emotion, the roads like winding pathways through a maze of apprehension. Our palms clung to each other, the connection serving as a lifeline amidst the uncertainty. As we walked through the hospital doors, I couldn't shake the sense that this was a pivotal moment, a crossroads where our journey would once again take a new direction. The familiar faces of the medical staff greeted us with a mix of compassion and urgency, their expertise a beacon of hope during the storm.

In the hours that followed, time seemed to both stretch and contract, bending to the rhythm of the waiting game. The operating room became a stage where a life-changing scene was set to unfold. As my wife was prepped for surgery, the symphony of beeping monitors and hushed voices played like a soundtrack to our hopes and fears. I stood by her side, my hand gripping hers, and we exchanged a glance that spoke volumes—a mixture of love, determination, and the shared knowledge that we were on the cusp of a new chapter in our story.

As the doors to the hospital room swung open, ushering her into a realm of medical expertise, I whispered a prayer—words woven with all the hope and longing that resided within me. In that moment, the future felt as fragile as a wisp of smoke, hanging in the balance between uncertainty and the unbreakable tether of our love. And so, we held on to hope, the very essence of what had carried us through this journey thus far, believing that no matter the outcome, our story was one of courage, resilience, and the extraordinary power of the human spirit.

Chapter 12

THE DAY HAS ARRIVED

November 2021:

The culmination of our odyssey drew near—a day that stood at the intersection of anticipation and trepidation, a crossroads between dreams and reality. With hearts brimming with hope and minds echoing with fervent prayers, my wife and I crossed the threshold of the operating room, poised to embrace the arrival of our daughter. The room itself seemed to radiate a soft glow; an aura woven from the threads of countless emotions. My wife, with a mixture of determination and vulnerability, settled onto the hospital bed, her grip on my hand a testament to the strength within her.

Hours stretched like taffy, each minute blending into the next as if time itself were under a spell. The steady rhythm of the heart monitor became a backdrop, a metronome to the symphony of labor and love. In that sacred cocoon of the delivery room, where pain and

51

anticipation intertwined, we navigated a journey that would etch its mark on our souls.

As I walked into the delivery room, my heart pounded like a drum, a symphony of nerves and excitement. My wife was being gracefully wheeled in via a gurney, her determined yet vulnerable expression mirrored my own whirlwind of emotions. Inside, the room bustled with activity - a carefully choreographed ballet of nurses and doctors, each with a specific role to play. My eyes were drawn to a table towards the back to the left, adorned with a pristine white sheet, but it wasn't the table that captured my attention. It was the team of four nurses, poised and ready, their eyes gleaming with a mix of professionalism and compassion. They were like guardian angels, armed not with wings, but with medical equipment and expertise. In that moment, any nervousness I felt was eclipsed by an overwhelming sense of trust in these skilled hands, entrusted with the most precious life of all - our daughter.

And then, as if the universe held its breath, the moment arrived—a moment that hung suspended in eternity. Our daughter's first cry pierced the air, a melody of life that resonated with the promise of new beginnings. Yet, before placing her in my arms, the nurses swiftly took her to ensure her well-being. With gentle urgency, they took her to that far table to the left, they checked her vitals, listened to her heartbeat, and ensured that she had transitioned into this world with the grace that befits a newborn. It was as if they held the strings of fate, gently orchestrating the symphony of her arrival.

As I witnessed her emergence, my heart swelled with a torrent of emotions that threatened to overflow. Tears streamed down my cheeks, borne of a joy so profound that it could not be contained. The nurses, with their unwavering expertise and tender care, cleared the path for this precious moment. And as they gently placed her in my arms, she became a living testament to the beauty of life's fragile beginnings.

Her eyes, still fresh from the otherworldly realm from which she had come, blinked open as if seeking to fathom the world she had just entered. Her tiny fingers curled around mine, a delicate touch that carried the weight of a lifetime of possibilities. In that transcendent moment, all the worries, doubts, and uncertainties that had shadowed our journey fell away like autumn leaves, leaving only the radiant glow of love in their wake. The room, once a backdrop of medical instruments and clinical routines, transformed into a sanctuary of profound connection. The vibrant energy in the air seemed to shimmer with a magic that transcended the mundane.

In that space of pure vulnerability and immeasurable strength, my wife and I shared a gaze that spoke volumes—a silent exchange of gratitude, wonder, and the unspoken promise to guide our daughter through the labyrinth of life. As the first rays of sunlight filtered through the window, bathing the room in a gentle warmth, our daughter nestled in my arms seemed to embody the very essence of a new day dawning. She was a testament to the resilience of the human spirit, a beacon of hope that had illuminated our path through darkness and uncertainty.

And so, as I cradled her tiny form, I admired the exquisite tapestry that had woven our lives together—the threads of struggle, triumph, and the fierce love that had carried us through. The journey was far from over, but as I looked into her eyes, I knew that every step, every twist, and every turn would be embraced with the same courage and love that had brought us to this moment. And as the world beyond the hospital room continued its ceaseless motion, we embarked on the next chapter of our story, welcoming our daughter GRACE into the world and guided by the radiant light of her arrival.

Chapter 13:

EMBRACING GRACE

In the wake of Grace's extraordinary arrival, the days that unfurled were a blend of profound joy and unwavering determination. The intricacies of caring for a newborn were magnified by the presence of her ventricular septal defect, trisomy 21, and the newly discovered challenge of conductive hearing loss. Our lives had been intricately woven into a tapestry of medical appointments, therapies, and moments of tender connection that whispered of the courageous journey we embark upon.

As the sun painted the horizon with hues of gold and rose, I often found myself gazing out the window, the quietude of dawn mirroring the stillness within my heart. The journey thus far had been marked by the ebb and flow of emotions, a symphony of highs and lows that danced to a rhythm only understood by those who had walked a similar path. I often traced the lines of her delicate features, my fingertips mapping the map of her resilience—the gentle curve of her nose, the flutter of her eyelashes, and the soft rise and fall of her chest as she slept, a testament to her unwavering spirit.

Our days were now punctuated by the music of medical equipment—the soft hum of monitors, the rhythmic beeping of machines. Yet, amidst this symphony of medical necessity, there emerged a song of profound love and boundless hope. With every feeding, every diaper change, and every therapy session, we poured our hearts into ensuring that she felt the warmth of our presence, the cocoon of security that only a parent can provide.

The journey was not without its challenges. The weight of the diagnoses we carried was at times overwhelming, casting shadows of doubt and fear. But in those moments, we turned to the beacon of light that had guided us thus far—the grace of God and the strength of our daughter's spirit. She had an uncanny ability to infuse every room she entered with an aura of joy, her eyes sparkling with curiosity and her infectious laughter resonating like a melody of hope. Amidst the whirlwind of appointments and therapies, we discovered the incredible strength that resided not only within us, but within Grace. The bond between my wife and I deepened, each challenge reinforcing our partnership and reminding us of the unbreakable love that had brought us to this point. We embraced the mantra that had carried us through the storm—every obstacle was an opportunity to grow, every setback was a chance to learn, and every moment was a gift to be cherished.

Through every twist and turn of our journey, our daughter's tenacity shone like a beacon, a guiding light through the darkest of times. She tackles each therapy session, every doctor's appointment with a fierce determination that seems to defy her tender age. Even during daunting medical procedures, her infectious joy remained undiminished. Her eyes, so full of hope and resilience, locked onto ours as if to declare, 'I'm here, and I'm ready for whatever comes my way'. Her spirit, indefatigable and unyielding, became a living testament to the boundless strength of the human heart.

Yet, while her courage illuminates our path, a shadow of uncertainty lingered. The doctors continue to closely monitor the tiny, precious heart that held our hopes and dreams. The possibility of heart surgery has not been ruled out, an unspoken fear that we carry in our hearts. But, amidst the turbulence of emotions, we cling to our faith, unwavering in our belief that everything would be okay. Our prayers became a lifeline, connecting us to a wellspring of hope. Our story was far from over, and with each passing day, it unfolded with both challenges and triumphs, a testament to the remarkable resilience of the human spirit.

As I cradled her in my arms, her tiny hand gripping my finger, I marveled at the resilience that had emerged from the trials we had faced. Our daughter was not defined by her medical conditions; she was defined by her spirit, her ability to spread love and light wherever she went. In her, we found hope, a living embodiment of grace that illuminated our lives with a brilliance that could not be dimmed by any challenge.

And so, in the quiet moments of the night, when the world around us was hushed in slumber, I held her close and whispered promises of love and unwavering support. We were no longer merely navigating the storm; we were dancing in the rain, embracing the challenges, and finding beauty amid adversity. The road ahead remains uncertain, as we continue this journey, but with each step, we are guided by the grace that had brought us this far—one that had transformed our lives into a testament of faith, hope, and the unyielding power of love.

Epilogue:

THE UNSEEN THREADS

In the quiet moments of reflection, as the tapestry of our journey unfurls before me, I am reminded that life's most profound stories are not just written in the grand gestures and epic battles. They are woven in the intricate details, the unexpected turns, and the resilience found in the creases of our hearts. Ours is a story of unforeseen threads that, when woven together, create a fabric rich with the hues of love, faith, and hope.

From the frosty embrace of that chilly spring night to the daunting battles with both an invisible virus and the unknown path of parenting an imperfect child, our journey has been a mosaic of emotions and experiences. It's as if fate has handed us a palette of colors, ranging from the brightest highs to the deepest lows, and challenged us to paint a canvas that is uniquely ours.

Our daughter's announcement of her pregnancy, a tale of youthful hope, was quickly followed by the revelation that my wife, my steadfast partner through life's rollercoaster, was expecting as well. In those moments, the universe seemed to whisper secrets of continuity and new beginnings. Life was embracing us in its most raw and exquisite form, inviting us to dance to a melody that resonated with both our fears and our dreams.

The doctor's call, laden with heavy uncertainties, was the crossroads where our story could have taken a different turn. The challenges outlined could have overwhelmed us, but in that pivotal instant, we chose the path less traveled. We chose to walk alongside our daughter, to embrace our unborn child, regardless of the hurdles that awaited us. It was as if our decision had breathed new life into the threads of our existence, weaving resilience into the very fabric of our family.

Grace's journey, one fraught with uncertainty and vulnerability, unfolded in parallel with my own path towards recovery. Two intertwined narratives of growth and transformation, each with its unique battles and victories. As my strength was reclaimed from the clutches of illness, I witnessed the beauty of resilience mirrored in my daughter's determination to face life's challenges head-on. Her imperfections, beautifully imperfect, became an anthem to the unyielding spirit within us all. In navigating uncharted waters, she bestowed upon us the precious gift of grace, a reminder that strength flourishes in embracing the imperfect, a beacon of quiet courage lighting our way.

In our epilogue, as in life, there is no neatly tied bow that signifies an end. Rather, it's a pause—a moment to catch our breath and marvel at the beauty of the journey. Our path forward is a continuation, an unfolding narrative that will be shaped by unforeseen threads, each adding depth and dimension to our story.

And so, with hearts brimming with gratitude, we step forward, our hands intertwined, ready to face whatever the unwritten chapters of our story may hold. As the threads of our lives continue to weave together, I am certain of one thing—the beauty of our journey lies not just in its destination, but in every step we take, in every moment we cherish, and in every thread that

connects us to the profound tapestry of life –
guided by the……

Grace

of

God

 @gracies_journey

 @ourjourneywithgrace

www.ingramcontent.com/pod-product-compliance
Lightning Source LLC
Chambersburg PA
CBHW050612160726
48003CB00003B/1157